IS IT REALLY MY BEDTIME?

EULLA GRACE

Dedication

I dedicate this book to all the little children in my life who bring happiness and joy to my heart every time I see them. I love them all. xx

Acknowledgment

A big thank you to my family for supporting me and to my dear mum for pushing me to write a book. I also express my gratitude to the publishers for their support, creativity and guidance.

About the Author

This is my second children's book, which I have greatly enjoyed writing. I hope this story brings a sense of calm for children at bedtime

Is it really bedtime?
But I just want to play!
I have been so very busy
But I've had a lovely day

Mummy carries me to bed
My little legs are sleepy too
She gets my stories ready
And reads me just a few

She sees my eyes are tired
As I snuggle in her arm
She reads so very softly
And very, very calm

I tell Mummy I'm not tired
But as she switches off the light
I fall asleep, so content
And she kisses me goodnight

Good sleep is important
For our bodies and minds

So we can learn with our brain
And enjoy things of all kinds

www.ingramcontent.com/pod-product-compliance
Lightning Source LLC
Chambersburg PA
CBHW041731140626
46547CB00026BA/519